PROCEEDINGS

OF THE

THURSDAY-EVENING CLUB,

On the Occasion of the Death

OF

HON. EDWARD EVERETT.

BOSTON:
WILSON AND SON, PRINTERS.
1865.

EDWARD EVERETT

DIED ON THE 15TH OF JANUARY, A.D. 1865,

AGED 71.

At a meeting of the THURSDAY-EVENING CLUB, on January 26, 1865, at the house of Mr. GARDNER BREWER, it was agreed, in accordance with a resolution offered by Hon. G. WASHINGTON WARREN, that the remarks made that evening, on the occasion of the death of Mr. EVERETT, should, with the consent of his family, be printed for private distribution among the members.

PROCEEDINGS

OF THE

THURSDAY-EVENING CLUB.

DR. WARREN'S REMARKS.

Gentlemen, — Since the last meeting of this Club, death has visited us; and, in the person of our friend and President, has called away the first citizen of our Commonwealth.

Honored alike at home and abroad, his loss will be felt throughout the length and breadth of the civilized world; and his name will justly stand among the most distinguished of all ages.

Again and again, during the last week, has his eulogy been pronounced, in terms far more adequate to his merits than any which I can employ; yet here, in this circle of friends, we once more contemplate him in the private and social relation which he bore to this Association.

The peculiar organization of our Club — designed (to use the words of Mr. Everett, as spoken here on a former occasion) to bring together persons of different professions and pursuits, to converse and communicate with each other on the scientific improvements of the day, and other topics connected with social culture and progress; thus uniting the active and the professional, the scientific and business classes of the community in a friendly circle — has been successful, in no common degree, in combining refined social enjoyment with mutual improvement in knowledge.

The objects of such an association were fully appreciated by Mr. Everett; and, from the very commencement of its meetings, his polished eloquence and rare conversational powers have greatly contributed to its success. Especially to be remembered are the noble eulogies in which he commemorated the removal by death of several prominent members of our Club; and we all remember, with gratitude and admiration, the splendid tribute, which, on the late decease of Mr. Frederic Tudor, he paid to the memory of the friend at whose house, only two weeks before, we had been so hospitably entertained. His illustrations of literary and historical subjects, with which he constantly favored us, are among the happiest reminiscences of our meetings; always felicitous in themselves, and often doubly impressive as emanating from one who had himself been an actor in the scenes which he described.

The first meeting of this season was held at his house, on the anniversary of the landing of our pilgrim forefathers; and, in a style clear and masterly, even beyond his usual manner, he drew a new and vivid picture of that humble beginning of our national existence. Only a fortnight ago to-day, I received a note from him, regretting much that he was unable, owing to what he thought a slight illness, to be present at the meeting of that evening.

Of the punctuality with which, as President of the Club, he opened the meetings, you are all aware; for he well knew the value of time when measured by such results as he was accustomed to attain.

Feeling myself entirely incapable of doing justice to an occasion like this, I have yet been unwilling to let the evening pass without adding my feeble testimony to his entire faithfulness as a member and presiding officer of this Association. I leave to a gifted member of our Club the grateful task of giving fit expression to our sense of the great loss which we have sustained.

Mr. Whipple said: —

It is certainly fit, gentlemen, that the sense of bereavement which this city and the whole nation have felt in the death of Mr. Everett, should find emphatic expression in the Club of which he was the honored President. Known to every member as the most exquisitely affable of presiding officers; a chairman with the gracious and graceful manners of a host; ever ready to listen as to speak; and masking the eminence, which all were glad to acknowledge, in that bland and benignant courtesy, of which all were made to feel the charm,—his presence gave a peculiar dignity to our meetings which it will be impossible to replace, and impressed on all of us the conviction, that, to his other gifts and accomplishments, must be added the distinction of being the most accomplished gentleman of his time. Indeed, it is probable, that, in this quality of high-bred and inbred courtesy, which we all have such good cause to admire and to remember, may be found the explanation and justification of some things in his character and career which have been subjected to adverse and acrimonious criticism; and, in the few remarks I propose to make, allow me to throw into relations to this felicity of his nature, the powers and achievements which have made him so widely famous, and, what is better, so widely mourned.

Mr. Everett was born with that fineness of mental and of bodily organization, the sensitiveness of which is hardly yet thoroughly tolerated by the world which still profits by its superiorities. There was refinement in the very substance of his being; by a necessity of his constitution he disposed every thing he perceived into some orderly relations to ideas of dignity and grace; he instinctively shunned what was coarse, discordant, uncomely, unbecoming; and that internal world of thoughts, sentiments, and dispositions, which each man forms or re-forms for himself, and in which he really lives, in his case obeyed the law of comeliness, and came out as naturally in his manners as in his writings, in the beautiful urbanity of his behavior as in the cadenced periods of his eloquence. The fascination of this must have been felt even in his childhood, — for he was an orator whose infant prattle attracted an audience; and he may be said to have passed from the cradle into public life. To a swiftness and accuracy of apprehension which made study the most delightful and self-rewarding of tasks, he added a general brightness, vigor and poise of faculties, which gave premature promise of the reflection and judgment which were to come. By some sure instinct, the friends who seemed combined in a kindly conspiracy to assist and to spoil him, must have felt that they had to do with a nature whose innate modesty was its protection from conceit, and whose ambition to excel was but one form of its ambition for excellence. The fact to be considered is, that, in childhood and in youth as in manhood and age, there was something in him which irresistibly attracted admiration and esteem, and made men desirous of helping him on *in* the path his genius chose, and *to* the goal from which his destiny beckoned.

It will be impossible here to do more than indicate the steps of that comprehensive career, so full of distinction for himself, so full of benefit to the nation, which has been for the past ten days the theme of so many eulogies: — the college student, bearing away the highest honors of his class; the boy-preacher, whose pulpit eloquence alternately kindled and melted men of maturest years; the Greek Professor, whose knowledge of the finest and most flexible instrument of human thought extorted the admiration of the most accomplished of all the translators of Plato; the fertile Writer and wide-ranging Critic, whose familiarity with many languages only added to the energy and elegance with which he wielded the resources of his own; the Representative of Middlesex, whose mastery of the minutest details of political business was not more evident than his ready grasp of the broader principles of political science; the Governor of Massachusetts, whose wise and able administration gave a new impulse to the cause of education and to some of the most important of the arts of peace; the Ambassador, who co-operated with his friend, the great Secretary, in converting the provocations to what would have been one of the most calamitous of all wars into the occasion for negotiating one of the most beneficent of all treaties; the President of Harvard, bringing back to his *Alma Mater* the culture he had received from her increased an hundred fold, and presenting to the students the noble example of a scholarship which was always teaching, and therefore always learning; the Secretary of State, whose brief possession of office was yet sufficient to show with what firmness of purpose he could uphold American honor, and with what prodigality of information he could expound American rights; the Orator of all "occasions," scattering through many years, and from a hundred platforms, the rich stores of his varied knowledge, the ripe results of his large experience, and the animating inspirations of his fervid soul; the Patriot, who ever made his scholarship, statesmanship, and eloquence serviceable and subsidiary to the interest and glory of his country, and who, when would-be parricides lifted their daggers to stab the august mother who had borne them, flung himself, with a grand superiority to party prejudices, and a brave disdain of consequences to himself, into the great current of impassioned purpose which surged up from the nation's heroic heart; the Christian philanthropist, who, through a long life, had been the object of no insult or wrong which could rouse in him the fierce desire for vengeance, and whose last public effort was a magnanimous plea for that "retaliation" which Christianity both allows and enjoins: — all these claims to honor, all this multiform and multiplied activity, have been the subjects of eager and emulous panegyric; and little has been overlooked in the loving and grateful survey.

Such a career implies the most assiduous self-culture; but it was a culture free from the fault of intellectual selfishness, for it was not centred in itself, but pursued with a view to the public service; and the thirst for acquisition was not stronger than the ardor for communication. Such a career also implies a constant state of preparation for public duties; but only by those whose ambition is to get office, rather than to get qualified for office, will this peculiarity be sneeringly imputed to a love of display. Still, the vast publicity which such a career rendered inevitable would have developed in him some of the malignant or some of the frivolous vices of public life, had it not been that a fine modesty tempered his constant sense of personal efficiency, — had it not been that a certain shyness at the core of his being made it impossible that his self-reliance should rush rudely out in any of the brazen forms of self-assertion.

And this brings me back to that essential gentlemanliness of nature, which penetrated every faculty, and lent its tone to every expression, of our departed President. This gave him a most sensitive regard for the rights and feelings of others, and this made him instinctively expect the same regard for his own. He guarded with an almost jealous vigilance the reserves of his individuality, and resented all uncouth or unwarranted intrusion into these sanctuaries which his dignity shielded, with a feeling of grieved surprise. In his wide converse with men, even in the contentions of party, his mind ever moved in a certain ideal region of mutual courtesy and respect. It was to be anticipated, that, in the rough game of politics, where blows are commonly given and received with equal carelessness, and where mutual charges of dishonesty are both expected and unheeded, such a nature as Mr. Everett's should sometimes suffer exquisite pain; that his nerves should quiver in impatient disgust of such odious publicity; that he should be tempted at times to feel that the inconsiderate assailers of his character —

"Made it seem more sweet to be
The little life of bank and brier,
The bird that pipes his lone desire,
And dies unheard within his tree,

"Than he who warbles long and loud,
And drops at Glory's temple-gates;
For whom the carrion-vulture waits
To tear his heart before the crowd!"

In this sensitiveness, refinement, and courtesy of nature, in this chivalrous respect for other minds, and tenderness for other hearts, is to be found the peculiarity of his oratory. He was the last great master of persuasive eloquence. The circumstances of the time have given to our public speaking an aggressive and denouncing character, and invective has contemptuously cast persuasion aside, and almost reduced it to the condition of one of the lost arts. This is undoubtedly a great evil, for invective commonly dispenses with insight, is impotent to interpret what it assails, and fits the tongue of mediocrity as readily as that of genius. It is true that the mightiest exemplars of eloquence have been those who have wielded this most terrific weapon in the armory of the orator with the most overwhelming effect. Demosthenes, Chatham, Burke, Mirabeau, men of vivid minds, hot hearts, and audacious wills, have made themselves the terror of the assemblies they ruled, by their power of uttering those brief and dreadful invectives, which "appal the guilty and make bold the free," — which come like the lightning, irradiating *for* an instant what *in* an instant they blast. Perhaps the noblest spectacle in the annals of eloquence is that in which the mute rage and despair of a hundred millions of Asiatics found, in the assembly responsible for their oppression, fiery utterance from the intrepid lips of Burke. But such men are rightly examples only to their peers; a certain autocracy of nature is the animating principle of their genius; and, when they are copied simply by the tongue, they are likely to produce shrews rather than sages. Mr. Everett followed the bent of his character and the law of his mind when he aimed to enter into genial relations with his auditors, and to associate the reception of his views with a quickening of their better feelings, and an addition to their self-respect. Mount Vernon, the poor of East Tennessee, the poor of Savannah, attest that his greatest triumphs were those of persuasion. And in recalling the tones of that melodious voice, whose words were thus works, one is tempted to think that Force, in eloquence, is the mailed giant of the feudal age, who, assailing under a storm of missiles the fortress of his adversary, makes the tough gates shiver under the furiously rapid strokes of his battle-axe, and enters as a victor; while Persuasion, "with his garland and singing robes about him," speaks the magical word which makes the gates fly open of their own accord, and enters as a guest.

It is but just, gentlemen, that our lamented President, the source of so many eulogies, should now be their theme; that his joy in recognizing eminency in others should be met by a glad and universal recognition of it in himself. And, certainly, that spotless private and distinguished public life could have closed at no period when the heart of the whole loyal nation was more eager to admire the genius of the orator, and sound the praises of the patriot, and laud the virtues of the man, than on the day when his mortal frame, beautiful in life and beautiful in death, was followed by that long procession of bereaved citizens, through those mourning streets, to that consecrated grave!

Bishop EASTBURN said: —

I ask the indulgence of my fellow-members of the Club for a few moments, while I add to the eloquent words that have been spoken my own humble tribute to the memory of our late illustrious President. Mr. Everett was kind enough once to say to me, that he wished I would sometimes offer something, at these meetings, as a contribution towards the instruction of those who should be present. My reply to him was, that, surrounded as I always found myself here by so much science and wisdom, I felt disposed rather to sit as a silent listener; and I cannot help a solemn and tender feeling in the reflection, that when now, for the first time, I am complying with his request, it is to utter a few words of remembrance over his recently opened grave.

I beg to call your attention, gentlemen, in the few words I shall say, to one or two points in Mr. Everett's illustrious career which have not been dwelt upon by the speakers who have just addressed us,—and which seem to me to present him in an aspect eminently worthy of study by the rising youth of this nation.

I very often thought, during the life of our distinguished President, and have thought more especially since his death, of the shining example he has set of the assiduous cultivation of classical learning, as the chief ingredient in efficient education, and as the great means of giving superior abilities a commanding influence over men. It was this that gave the charm to Mr. Everett's oratory, and carried home with power his advocacy, as a statesman, of public measures, and his addresses in behalf of those efforts for the relief of suffering humanity to which he devoted the closing years of his life. He seemed to enter fully into those views of the advantage of classical pursuits put forth by the great Sir Robert Peel, in a discourse delivered by him on being installed as Lord Rector of the University of Glasgow, and which I remember reading many years ago,—where he speaks of the benefits of classical, as distinguished from mere mathematical training; and shows the tendency of the latter to narrow the mind, and to indispose it, in regard to a certain class of subjects, to receive any other than a species of evidence of which these subjects are not susceptible. But, besides this, Sir Robert exhibited, in a striking manner, the inestimable value of the study of the great masters, by a review of the course of Cicero, whose wonderful oratory received its perfection, and its power of swaying men, from his cultivation of the great models of Grecian poetry and eloquence. Now Mr. Everett, as I have said, is a great example in this respect, and ought to be held up as such before the young men of this land. And, if he shall be generally followed, we shall hear less, in the pulpit, on the platform, and on deliberative floors, of that rant and bombast which pass with some for eloquence, but which are as offensive to good taste as they are barren of effect. Mr. Bullock, in his address at Faneuil Hall on the day before the funeral of our departed President, dwelt with great force and eloquence upon this way in which Mr. Everett trained himself for influence,—showing that his classical finish was not something standing by itself, and apart from his distinction as a statesman, but was the main element in creating that distinction, and in giving him the power which he possessed in his signal public career. And, gentlemen, who has not felt the control exerted by his brilliant, yet restrained, chastened, and simple diction? His oratory, sparkling with ornament as it was, was at the same time a perfect specimen of the *simplex munditiis*. So that, whenever we heard him, it was like looking at some noble Grecian temple, in the presence of which the eye is not distracted hither and thither by tawdry and vulgar details, but takes in at once the exquisite *whole*, and is charmed with the beauty of its architectural lines, and the fair symmetry of its proportions.

But, before I sit down, allow me to detain you for a few moments longer by reminding you of another feature of Mr. Everett's career, which ought to be impressed on the youth of this country. I refer to the fact, that this great man achieved his triumphs, and produced the results which we have witnessed, by a life of constant and laborious industry. He eminently taught by his example, that they who would either attain eminence, or, what is infinitely more important, would urge mankind onward to noble purposes, must not rely upon the native genius with which God has gifted them, but must discipline their faculties by unremitted labour. My first sight of Mr. Everett was forty-three years ago, when, in 1822, he came to New York to deliver the Sermon at the opening of a place of worship of his denomination. I had not then entered on my own professional course; and, with the curiosity and enthusiasm of a youth desirous of getting a near sight of so eminent a man,—for even then he was eminent, although but twenty-eight years of age,—I took a position, after the service was over, in the porch, in order that I might study his countenance as he passed out into the street:—and, as he walked by me with his slender form, in gown and band, with his curling auburn hair, and his fine contour of head and features, I thought him the most attractive specimen of radiant classical beauty I had ever beheld in my life. Now, gentlemen, many of us have been witnesses of his course from that morning of his life down to its recent close. And what has this course been? Has it been an indolent resting upon the consciousness of great natural endowments? No. Has it been a course marked by fitful and impulsive resort to study? No. It has been a life of unintermitted labour—of continual storing of the mind—of daily addition to that wealth of resources which was to be the instrument of power. I have touched upon this feature of Mr. Everett's distinguished life, because, as I have already observed, I think it should be placed distinctly before the young men of this country; showing them for their instruction, that influence, and consequent usefulness, come not from intellect alone, however marvellous, but from intellect disciplined, regulated, and made efficient, by the toil which 'scorns delights, and lives laborious days.'

I thank you for the permission to present these thoughts to your attention; for I felt that I could not refrain from adding my humble tribute to this remarkable man, here in one of those assemblies which he has so often adorned with his presence, and charmed with the contributions of his eloquent lips.

Dr. A. A. Gould said, —

I am sure that each one of us here associated must feel thankful to the gentlemen who have so faithfully and gratefully delineated the exalted character of our late President, and especially as they recall to us his interest in our meetings, and the many contributions he himself made for our entertainment and edification. The breaking out of the rebellion bore so heavily on his health and spirits, that he expressed some misgivings as to his ability to meet with us, and even as to the judiciousness of continuing the meetings of the Club. At the preliminary meeting this year, however, he seemed quite enthusiastic in view of our coming entertainments; and you will all of you attest to the peculiar geniality with which he opened our winter's gatherings at his own house.

I venture to propose, what I have no doubt will find an affirmative response from every one, that the gentlemen who have addressed us be requested to furnish copies of their remarks, to be transmitted to the family of our late President, as a testimonial, from the members of this Club, of their deep sense of indebtedness to him for his countenance, and his numerous instructive and entertaining contributions at their meetings, as well as of his exalted private worth and public eminence.

www.ingramcontent.com/pod-product-compliance
Lightning Source LLC
LaVergne TN
LVHW011146110826
845150LV00008B/2545

* 9 7 8 1 4 1 8 1 9 1 7 6 4 *